TILTH

For Lisa Steppe

TILTH

Peggie Gallagher

ARLEN
HOUSE

TILTH

is published in 2013 by
ARLEN HOUSE
42 Grange Abbey Road
Baldoyle
Dublin 13
Ireland
Phone/Fax: 353 86 8207617
Email: arlenhouse@gmail.com

Distributed internationally by
SYRACUSE UNIVERSITY PRESS
621 Skytop Road, Suite 110
Syracuse, NY 13244–5290
Phone: 315–443–5534/Fax: 315–443–5545
Email: supress@syr.edu

ISBN 978–1–85132–072–1, paperback

Typesetting ¦ Arlen House
Cover Image ¦ 'Henry's Sebright'
by Elaine Garvey

Tilth won the 2011 Listowel Writers' Week Poetry Collection
Award, sponsored by Profile Developments, Glin, Co Limerick.

CONTENTS

TILTH

LANDFALL

When the gale is spent,
when darkness empties,
yields to a brightening scrim,

and a blade of dim brilliance
turns its edge on the horizon,
opens a seam on the sea's teal,

a sheet of lit syllables,
a glittering disrememberance
of the night's pitch and heave;

the growing light probes
its salted hallways, its foam
white as our ancestors' bones

that roam its lanes and byways
cold and mindless
touching the waves blindly.

But look
– the sea moves her mirrors,
land swims at lit intervals,

steady-keeled, our battered craft,
rank with fish stink and diesel,
slices a wake toward the headland.

An uncontrollable tremor;
light spills through the shoulder
of the limestone shore.

ATLANTIS

The cusp of summer, the ocean spread before us,
a lavish interlude of blue.
Think how this was once our element,
our kelp-scented breast.

How we plunged into its cisterns,
earth creatures naked and luminous,
surfacing to the sound of gulls and gannets,
the never-settling terns picking at the surf.

And there, stretched above the village,
the stone-shouldered mountain
like a mythic keeled-up ship,
a fable we might enter,

a cavern bearing our hieroglyphs,
scattered calc and bone fragments,
two effigies wrapped in linen,
a table laid with sea thrift.

HIEROGLYPHS

This morning I woke to find a blue tit
chiselling a seam on the curve of my cheek,
spiky feet prickling the skin of my chin,

his hot-needle beak like a sewing machine
running laps between my nose
and the swerve of my ear,

then tightening his grip with a hiss and tick
of his wings, his relentless nib
whipstitches the quick of my lips.

In the interest of symmetry, he continues
to barb-link my twin cheek,
finishing with a sting of his initials.

All day my fingers track a faint alphabet,
a vanishing language of claw prints.

EQUINOX

Dawn of ice-blue light
    a full moon holds sway
        above the pines

I am drawn outside
    to stand in the frost-licked grass
        lift my eyes to the sky

streaming in from the east
    a school of rooks rises
        in great loose skeins

they blend and skim
    spin high and wide
        into the brightening light

loop back on themselves
    switch and slip
        from pattern to pattern

above the horizon
    their call barely audible
        wanting nothing more

than this vast sky
    this shining vantage point
        a sheet of stars

shape-shifting
    wave after wave
        as the planets balance

EBB AND FLOW

On the fray of tide
amid sea-wrack and razor-shell
lies the full stretch of your life
your small body stilled
a bone-work torso
from haunch to delicate forepaw

sand shifts
as the rocking waves
unstitch
your handful of days

your skull stripped clean
a christening cup
a receptacle
the sea enters
and leaves

on a ridge of kelp
and splinter shells
and the moon
trawling her wide acres
gathers you back to her bed

EARTHWORM

Think how it panics
on the gravel drive,
twisting and turning,

burning for the cold underside
of stone, a dark planet,
a moist blanket of soil.

How it shrinks and lengthens
each centimetre
of its thin blind skin.

A reddish-pink scribble
pointing its nose
for the slightest fissure

in flint, an interstice,
a bolt-hole,
a lost poem of home.

How quickly a day can change:
one moment you're rummaging alone
in the vast pocket of the dark,

dilating and bloating through loam.
The pleasures here
are well known,

and there's no richer pudding
plumped to bursting
with finds:

an ear, a wing, the satin eye
of a butterfly, moonseeds under a leaf,
fretwork of a millipede,

and once
on a tuft of mud
the scarlet husk of a ladybird.

PENINSULA

The day you died I carried you back
on a catch of breath.
I stood by
a long way off on a rock,
on a rooftop made of glass.

You had the air of someone taking stock
before a long journey,
staring into the limits of what could be seen,
the line between water and sky.

I watched the tide gift you a kiss
with soft sand.
Later, I walk across
a stippling of snail blue waves,

plunge into the melting place
under the ribcage,
that I might sleep in your salt scent
and wake in a land I have not seen.

THE RED HOUR
for Eíbhlín Evans

Risen from sleep with an urgency
beyond her knowing, the woman
fleshes onto canvas
the red
that has burned all night
in the furnace of her bones.

Fevered in that moment
when soul finds the body open,
pours itself through
in bold strokes;
a bouquet of carmine and ruby,
plum and scarlet,

as though she has breached
a gap in the horizon,
pried open its aorta,
a quickening river of magenta,
drowning in the cobalt
pick-up mirror of the sea.

AEOLIAN

How easy to make promises,
don't you know
memory is not mortal

and the wind is a gossip
that hoards a swarm of words,
and braided into the wind

are clear ocean sounds;
a yearning we cannot touch,
or reach for the words.

It is a house foundered,
a shell-like sound
that roars with silence.

It is a shoreline half-eaten by waves,
it is the same yearning that closes us,
opens us again.

DELOS

And so Leto, could this be the island
that takes pity on your plight? The floating island
of no fixed location in which to birth your twins,
safe from the vengeful queen, ox-eyed Hera
wanting to tear blue out of the story.

Zeus's seed pocketed inside you,
its ninth moon ripe and primal with birth pangs.
Now might your sisters, high on Olympus,
outwit the queen, bribe her midwife Eilithyia,
distract her with a splendid necklace,
that she would uncross her legs, let spill
the red blessings of your womb.

Oh exiled Leto, then would you sing
at the first wild sight of your children.

DAMSELFLY

Go, little damselfly, with your flicker of light
and spyglass eyes, and ferret out of the breeze
some template from the past, some entity
sifting under the bare bones of twigs.

Hover there, let the eye of your aqua stylus
unfurl its crumpled purse of hurt;
a faint current that ravels upwards,
all hum and hue to the tune of drifting things.

Bright *demoiselle*, you too must pursue your ends,
glean insects off leaves and webs, carry your eggs
to lake's edge, pierce stalk and blade.

In the wake of your flame, host-stems tremble
as though stung with a glittering pain.

THE BLUE SHELF

Stop looking for what lies behind
the glass mountain, Grandmother said.
But why? If, on a summer's day

the lake split-levels her gaze
to find Cairn's Hill immersed
head and shoulders in text

and the trees' sisterly whisperings,
peering down their bell-skirts
at the patina of their peep-toe selves,

their lived space portioned between horizons,
a blank pane that can flex with the sky.
Who then would say where Eden lies.

LETTER TO ELIZABETH

Each day with so much ceremony
  Begins, with birds ... Elizabeth Bishop

A pink translucence veils the hills.
Suspended on silk, a jet purrs toward Belfast.
Under ridged tiles and chimney-stacks,
red-bricks slumber belly to back
amid pylons and church spires.

Here come the gulls,
wheeling, sunrise tinting their breasts,
a shift of wing and they're earth-sweepers,
skimming, lifting, perching on cowls
snowy with droppings.

So absorbed in this
I almost miss
the woman who walks up an alley
in her nightdress.
A woman my age or less
this pink morning.

Something in the way she saunters
is as if she has just been kissed all over.

Not that you'd call her glamorous –
blonde, yes, (who isn't these days)
or that she's petite and sylphlike;
I can vouch for stout hips and thighs.

It's as if she is lit from within,
still nibbling the night's sweetmeats,
its almonds and figs, its wineskins
ripe with musky honey ...

Mulling over all this,
she caught me.
One sharp glance
sends me reeling back from the glass.

Makes you think about this lurking behind windows
waiting to trap the unwary image
this groping for metaphors
and finicky tinkering with metre and form.

INCOMMUNICADO

For a whole week the black handpiece
idles on its cradle, silent and cheerless
as a sullen teenager.

When it kicks back into action,
an avalanche of delayed messages
spill out its mouthpiece.

Here they come, stuttering down the line
like a deluge of damp leaves
from a backed-up down-pipe.

Seven days clinging to frayed filaments,
a hapless band of stranded messages
whose path has just vanished,

they cannot go forward
cannot go back.
What of their time in space,

their vantage point,
swinging like children
on the high wire?

The new neighbours,
did they settle for wallpaper
or paint?

That man with the stick,
who does he visit
every Wednesday?

Did they cheer unanimously
when the Eircom man from Dunfanaghy
located them on the wavering needle of his meter?

Useless to quiz them
as they shake themselves out on the kitchen floor.
They are like pilgrims or missionaries
intoning over and over the same old story.

PRIME

It is midwinter.
Your hands are chilled.
I lift you,
gather your first whimpers onto my pillow,
knowing as much by instinct as touch of skin.

We lie here amazed at the dark,
aware of the house sleeping around us,
the quiet patterns of breath.
Outside, the snow lies thick.

In this landscape of wild skies
and running tides,
and mornings lit with rapture,
I think

I must have been falling most of my life
to land here temple to temple
in this pre-dawn calm,
this kinship

of breath with breath
your hands cupped in my palms.

OMEN

And what was she to make of this morning,
her hand coming across
a clutch of fingernail clippings
in the pocket of a dress from America,

ten crescent wings,
each tiny sickle
intimate and anonymous

as the sweepings of a bird's nest
or tresses tossed on a convent floor.

Parlour

A bolthole, a room half elsewhere
adrift in distant grandeur,
where breath condenses between damask drapes
and the wing of a mahogany table.
Where an ear might catch the scratch
of a pen, a girl trawling the depths of an inkwell
pouring words, slippery as a river of fish
spilling loose of their net,
slapping their wet tails on the brocade.

What to do with such riches –
feed them to her mother's wedding gifts,
pile them into fluted dessert dishes,
fling their blue-black panic into the belly
of the lamp ravening on the sideboard,
the soft spill of innards silvering her fingers
cracking their verbs and consonants
the way her mother cracks
the necks of chickens.

THE UNMAKING

The air between us has grown dense
the roof leaks
buckled rafters

give way to wood-lice
and mildew eats the plaster
as happens with neglect

ivy shutters the light
the clock sharpens its teeth
on the chimney breast

waiting for the right time
the right frame of mind
silence brims with chirrings

trapped whispers
bone-brittle syllables
gathered to an absence

somewhere
a door
opens

then closes again

A Bog Hole

hidden
in heather
she stumbled into once,
dropped
like a shot
through its gullet,
sucked in
chest high,
winter cold
at her thighs.
Strong arms
dragged her up,
the sucking mouth
closed behind her
with a slap.

He was like that.

Straddled
across her,
he smiled,
praised,
dazed her
with promises
she half-believed.
Then
his body flailed
in a spasm of cold,
the hard set
of his shoulders,
square hands
adjusting his cuffs,
the amber red in his eyes.

MOUNTAIN

Fitful as a filly April canters in.
Splatter of primrose hoof-prints.
The young grass trembles.

Ice-age striations
track the mountain's great flank.
Mist moves like muslin
above its long, lean back.

In the house by the sheep-field
the woman remembers
the lamb born dead,
the silk of its afterbirth.

Light that bounces off galvanise
and rests on a wet flagstone.
The gold day that suddenly rides off
in a shower of hail.

FROM MY KITCHEN WINDOW

The cotoneaster the blackbirds feasted on,
crimson berries that lit the boundary wall,
they stripped its branches bare.

The day we buried you,
how cold the wall looked.
A robin spearing disturbed earth.

Birch leaves sun-spill
across the kitchen floor.
Light burns
through the heart of a rose.

An empty house
full of your face.

It was all red;
your blouse was red
with heels to match,
an Aran sweater stuffed
between your legs was red,
the front seat was red.

About the foetus,
nothing was ever said.

MADRIGAL

Regret nothing.
Not the days wasted,
the hours waiting,

the memories lost,
lodged in a place
you cannot locate.

Begin again.
Hang out on a street corner
under lamplight
and watch people go by.

Regret nothing.
Not even this night
sat here, waiting to get started,
to find a lead into something

that will take you on a night ride,
a place to pitch your tent,
watch flies dance in torchlight,
catch the first pale glimmer

of a story, a line, a madrigal,
a silver fish.

THE TWINS

They've been lying in state for days
side by side on wooden biers.
Petrified elderberry eyes, tiny
feet and petal ears, dead asleep.

Reverent in grey pelt, their next-of-kin,
aunts and uncles, restless cousins,
mothers with youngsters still-at-hip,
move in whispers round the twins.

The little kingdom brings its gifts:
the snail his silver ribbons lays
upon the hapless pair, spider suspends
its silk from tail to whisker tip.

Thus mourned, death's angel comes to pass
two martyrs, wreathed in their traps.

SEA VIOLET

We have little need of words, you and I,
on a day that throws no shadow,
we know this shore,
this theatre our hammering house,
sun chiselling through clouds.

I want to cheer, run,
sweep my tongue over this day,
the way your dog streaks the dunes, wheels
at the sound of your voice calling him to heel.

I stay by your side, fall into your rhythm.
Your back stiffens as I tell you
of a toddler in navy shorts,
a young mother and a June day.

And you tell me of porpoises dancing
offshore, where coral lies, and how
to recognise the coming and going of tides.

As though there were nowhere else to be,
I name this day, bite into its brine,
lean my head to its song,
its neap-tide, its hemline quilted
with stones, polished moons.

The Day You Married My Father

What were you thinking,
the sea of May running with all that hue,
when you crossed the mearin fence

and tracked grass rampant with wild garlic,
to where first light spilled on Barley Hill,
you lit a fire and burned your old clothes,

your past shed like a skin,
released to the air
to the scream of swifts.

Teach me to take from this
the open secret of seasons:

blackthorn's stripped canvas
baring itself for a brace of stars,

the heart's unscripted page,
the fire from which I came.

Rhea Silvia

It was when I drew water from the spring, I'd seen
three dark-skinned women discussing the weather,
looking up at the clouds, bruised-pearl and gun-
metal, at the hour when the war god is abroad.

Suddenly all my words were flattened,
crushed like broken stalks on flagstones.
The sage and rosemary grew on. In the stalls
stallions shook the hills with their trumpeting.

At birth they took my sons – suckled by a she-wolf.
Their grief cloth I soaked in an altar of birth-blood,
tempered it in a fire of winter stars, made
a breastplate braced across the heart, knowing

on the day, on the very spot where the javelin strikes
that note will echo, clear-cut as an infant's cry.

IN HER LATER YEARS

with evening shrunk
to a moth-beat,

what gladdens her
is the random setting

of mismatched delph
on the kitchen table.

Slowly and ceremoniously
she lifts cups and plates,

examines their base,
checks their place on the table,

sets them back
with a deft exactness.

Ordered and absorbed,
her delph ceremony

performed over and over,
cups, plates and glassware

lifted and swivelled at eye level
as if, for an instant,

a lens flickers, a glimpsed imprint
swims into vision

bringing a wild delight to her eyes.
Her lips tremble,

a faint whisper
rivers the skin of her neck,

a remnant of stem crystal
tilts in her bony fingers.

TELEPHONE POLE

Loveliest of trees you're not,
old spindle-spine, catching first light,
mottled with moss and birdlime
above the shrill of forsythia.

Tethered to duty. Strangely reassuring.
Casting your lines on the horizon,
catching sound as a sail catches wind,
your junction box strapped like a mandolin,
relics of plastic caught in your wings.

How alike we've become,
with little to recommend us but tenacity,
billeted here at fate's whimsy
sharing the same patch.

A figure at the window
tracing the changing seasons,
sun bowling shadows across the grass,
sky turning from peach to ecru to blue,
six goldfinches at the birdfeeder.

What a pair of grubbers we've become,
sloughing off our nocturnal smells,
the in and the out of breath,
the vast and chaotic nerve-ends,

the tug and pull of our lives,
heart the size of two clenched fists,
the needle constantly atremble
telling the world's story.
Old dream-catcher,

gauging every sigh, every rustle,
the high sharp cries in the night,
the elegies, love-songs and lullabies,
the christenings, nuptials and requiems.

Crouching on the knife-edge
spider swaddling her catch.
The way happiness can hang by a thread.

MEDITATION ON SNAILS

When washing lettuce
I'm always amazed
the way tiny snails
bid for escape, as if
their minuscule shells,
like flotation chambers,
buoy them up from the
depths, and what genius
of engineering
enables a snail
to scale the lip-of-
the-sink and chart
a shining path over
an ocean of chrome?
Horned and regal, a
luminous creature,
no bigger than an
olive pit, ferrying
its shell round the bend
of the tap. Look at
this one's hapless
sense of direction,
latching onto my wrist,
heading for the scrub-
land of my forearm.
Down here, see these, flushed
from a bunch of leaves,
swept into the gullet
of the plug hole, and
look; two more, moving
as if they know where
they're going, sliding
over the draining-
board, over its ribs

and watercourses.
Two refugees I
could crush as easy
as the severed heads
they fled. Or, I could
whisk and blend them with
oil and vinegar.

LUCK OF THE DRAW

My brother is up at first light
pacing the steady nail of his smoker's cough,
the hungry way he looks
at my leaving.

Late nights we play twenty-five.
It's February again, his sixtieth year.
Stories he slips between deals
I lift like souvenirs.

We play pieces of childhood.
I see father's hands when he deals the cards.
Hearts and diamonds the rickety-
planks we light on,

raking the pack
for the spangled jack,
stories he shrugs off
like what he says surprises him.

When he was young he had a future.
After that he had work.
Once I would tell my brother
how mother grieved when he left.

But what do I know
of his grief –
the guarded room in his head
borders he's crossed separately.

Here too is his story:
a family portrait
a china cabinet.
fridge big as a coffin.

At his kitchen table
cards fanned between us
bridges we cross
as night narrows behind us.

Dawn finds his garden sleeping
under a snow quilt. I leave
my footprints and take
his face with me.

SOLACE

In winter, he tells me,
the ground freezes six feet down.
Despite his years here,
how badly he's dressed for the weather;
his bare head
and wind-whipped trouser legs.

It was covered in snow
the day I flew in;
roof-grids and evergreens
layered and crisp and still,
and one white expanse
dotted with Christmas wreaths.

Today the wreaths lean
on spindle-sticks
above small cold monuments.

He's not come for a while.
It took weeks to get over the upset.

We cross and re-cross the same plots.
Three pine trees in a row, is how he remembers,
scanning the markers
across acres and acres of graves.

She's probably looking at us laughing,
saying the two dopes can't find me.

Yet, a blanched panic crosses his face.
When he finds her he smiles as though
the bitter wind is a kindness to him,
his own space alongside her granite nameplate.

OBLATION

Dawn finds you high on the mountain ledge.
Sheep scuttle into the scrub. They struggle
to anchor themselves on a skim of earth.
March light strikes the solitary pine,
a blade in its own slant of shadow.

From here, ringforts dimple the fields below,
green tiers scored with hedges,
and the shoreline scalloped
by the white bite of the sea,
wind-pitched cries of gulls.

Half-way to the cairn, your hand ponders
the stone you carry, a dense language
of minerals: feldspar, quartz, mica, schist.
A carnelian thread veins its smooth dome —
obdurate and blind, it drinks heat from your palm.

Suddenly the cairn,
bare in the stark northern light,
inured to the wind's attrition,
stone heaped on stone –
raised altar to a hungry god.

THE THREE CARD TRICK MAN
after a line by Tom Duddy

The reason I come here is not the horses, though
bookie shops abound and a litter of crushed slips.
It is always sunny and work is over for the weekend
and the girl in the red dress has just stepped out –

not exactly a carnival atmosphere, more
a thoroughfare of anticipation, the mood buoyant,
a painter's delight,
the air still holding the day's warmth.

There he is just off a side-street,
part of a circle hunched around a makeshift table.
The scrubbed nape,
an odour of soap and aftershave.

The picture steadies, the table is swept,
and the look when he turns to her
pales the red of her dress.

Impossible to say what passes between them –
a wager of innocent measure,
the small treacheries of love and its necessities.
Here I will leave them with everything still to play for.

RESONANCE

His flanks, his hands,
the tender cleft of chin,
heavy with sleep
and peace and ease

and I underneath
with fear,
but something tender too,
something near.

What fright rose in me
to test the dream,
fight the deep
the way a child fights sleep.

Yet, feeling his presence melt,
I strove to bring him back,
hold him,
kiss of skin on skin …

and heart, foolish heart,
turned and flowered again
as if there were no killing frost,
no winter.

WREATH

Pecking the last of the grain
rooks ransack the haggard.
A man shoulders hay to his cattle.
Three fields down,
light dazzles my eyes
snagged by a flight of starlings.
The coffin lifts with ease.
As if by some chicanery,
the coat fits me to a tee;
a coat with my name
written in white even-spaced letters.
We girls are to carry the coffin.
Father is dead
outside the house where I used to live.

Outside the house where I used to live
father is dead.
We girls are to carry the coffin.
Written in white even-spaced letters,
a coat with my name.
The coat fits me to a tee.
As if by some chicanery,
the coffin lifts with ease.
Snagged by a flight of starlings,
light dazzles my eyes.
Three fields down,
a man shoulders hay to his cattle.
Rooks ransack the haggard
pecking the last of the grain.

BREAKING STILL

You find me this last Sunday
before Christmas,
the cradle of your hands
turning my face toward the lake.

Sun washes the feet of holm oaks,
air crystal as a spring
bleeding true and bright
from the heart of a mountain.

Lake and silence,
oh my quiet father,
a weightless clarity
falling to either side of us.

Is this what you want to show me,
these white winter lights
hushed in swan-down,
the slow unwrapping of a lake's lullaby.

FOR THE BIRDS

Between Bleeker and Broadway
an old man breaks bread,

handful of crumbs
flung mid-air,
light bounces on light.

Low sun slants across his back,
a rack of bones in a purse of skin.

Anxious as a child, his face roams
the sky between skyscrapers.
Birds flood in,

downpour of wings, scrabble of beaks
devouring his Sabbath feast.

November strikes shadows it cannot reach.

VERGE

Driving the back way home,
silent and snow-blind,
the road plummets
below us.

Sun hangs motionless
and time dies in the silence:
we are scattered stones
dazzled on this ice-capped ridge.

Then how the mind's dark song
will trip-switch,
and the heart itself
becomes a creaking bridge

on which the road swings left
running toward the hill slope;
a quickening of the familiar
rendered lavish and richly cold.

The farm gate furred,
shimmering in its iron sting,
and *glory be,*
the high kite of the clothesline,

a snow-white camisole filtering light.

What I Keep

Your long fingers through my childhood hair,
bringing me an orange
in the dark of night.

I see your face when I look in the mirror.
Once I saw a photograph
of a young girl in a dark dress
wearing a long pearl necklace.
That was your mother my cousin said.

I've kept the image,
scraps of things you said,
the slender valleys between the bones
on the back of your hands,
and a plastic bag marked *Hospital Property.*

It held your vest
and crumpled night-dress.

I empty them out on the bathroom floor.
Dead skin cells float over the tiles.

COURTESY

An orderly crowd gathers.
I'm last to arrive.

She beckons me forward,
her coffin a distance away.

I wear odd socks,
no shoes.

She's propped up in her box,
looking lovely in fur,
hair freshly dressed.

How nice of you to come, she smiles,
positioning herself
comfortably upright.

We chat for a while.
It would be difficult to do otherwise.

CHEEK BY JOWL

Say it is August with hours to squander
and the Belfast hills range shoulder
to shoulder in the near blue distance.
Say the laughter of children,
or the dog, or naïve curiosity
causes you to wander towards a green

triangle framed in tarmac, green
once perhaps, bleached now as a child's
abandoned sandal. A little girl's curiosity:
Does your dog bite? In the near distance
gable ends rise shoulder to shoulder,
murals bold and unsparing as squandered

paint-boxes, though careful as a child
keeping inside the lines; a curious
mix of emblems, soldiers in tan and green
camouflage, rifles raised shoulder
high. A flag whirls in the distance.
Young boys with time to squander

play cards round a garden table. Shoulders
tense. Silence suspends the distance
between them, then bursts into cheers, their green
beer-cans raised, squandered
tab-ends tossed to a flock of pigeons. Children
giggle, shout *Hello Jim* to a pale-faced, curious

man who patrols the narrow shoulder,
busies himself back and forth the green,
keeping an eye but never meeting an eye. Distant
curtains flicker. Above a lintel a squandered
red hand, open-palmed. The dog shivers, the curious
and terrible trust of a child

in her eyes, the lead slack on her shoulder.
Something stirs in the blood, the curious
reel begins to play backwards; distant
pictures, pigments of purple, green
and red. The crucified Christ and squandered
blood of martyrs who died for me when I was a child.

Keep to the green sing the little children.
The curious man has time to squander
and distant hills ring shoulder to shoulder.

HER OWN SELF

With the rapt concentration of a musician
she sits on the kitchen floor lidding and un-
lidding saucepans, switching them back
and over. Gleaming aluminium
swivels in her dimpled fists, cymbal-crashing
the dancing lids. Deep in her task,
steadfast in the purity of instinct,
the chink that's see-through to somewhere else.

This is her silver kingdom, the risen song of herself
through the washed rooms of the senses.
Jewels flash up from the dancing lids
catching glints and splinters of the kitchen,
a prism of her mammy at the sink,
off-centre daddy spins in her small fierce fists.

EARLY DELIVERY

What had us on the road
that early May morning
when the Ballisodare bread van
slalomed past
and dropped
two wax-wrapped, sliced-pans
on the tarmac
warm and fragrant
as two babies
tossed from their cradle.

The van sped on
swing-doors unbolted
like a run-away train
or a liberated pony
lifting its tail.

OLD LADY
Mormo maura

At the shadow hour of an August morning,
you slip in, your tired head settles
on fresh linen I have just gathered.

When trees and chimneypots have begun
to shoulder themselves free of dark,
I pause amid lingering night scents,

an alchemy of musk, mineral and rotting litter,
haunt of night creatures, their lusts and hungers,
the inscrutable hedgehog hoovering up slugs

and woodlouse, imagine! the thousands of mouths!
The honeydew and sap from damaged
branches that form your larder.

From what dark star do you take your bearings,
lifted and blown above ranks of nettles,
wings snagged now and then on spider nets,

the way my own thoughts catch and stagger
on small blows of memory.
There – a first twitter,

a feathered song that knows seasons by heart
any day now frantic chatter will signal
the flocks' retreat.

Ah! but you have already succumbed to sleep,
the bloom of night on your wings, closed
like a folded cloak, garment of mute hues,

brown ambers and slate, sable and powder greys,
a mottled and shadowed language
that mimics the dying leaves.

Yet, this morning's sun is a deeper gold,
more glowing, more burnishing
on dock stems and thistle heads,

light shafts trace more delicately
this moment, this bonus of decay.
this turning page.

The Magician

You're here again.
With a flick of the wrist
you throw the switch on your own wake.

The dresser dense and pitted with age.
Candles flicker against the window nets.
The polished coffin on its make-shift trestle.

Same scatter of neighbours and long-
dead relatives, their susurrus of prayers.
Here's the part you like best:

The way the grandchildren clamour in
trailing the guttery muck from the cow's drain –
hard to tell fear from excitement
on their clear morning faces.
What is it? you ask. The air stills.
Three sets of wellies move to the box.

They're anxious to tell you, bring you the news,
spilling out words like shining coins; the cow, the calf,
the shimmering, slithering river, the red-stained veil,

the heft and bellow of birth, its livid chrism.
The silk-sleeved calf staggering to its feet.
And Grandad, she licked him and licked him and licked him.

THRESHOLD

The scraw yields
easy as peeling back a blanket,
a story stirring in its sleep

as light slides in, the exposed tilth
falls open, dark and friable
with a talc of sand.

Lean into its earth smell,
to the well-thumbed script
of the last tenant.

Take up the cursive, its open tense,
the sifted diction
of what was once familiar.

And does it matter that the known
and the unknown touch
like the seep of music through bone

or that the story goes on telling
in a child's shoe
a mud-stained shell of leather,

crumpled, though still wearable
as if a small foot escaped
racing back across the grass.

ABOUT THE AUTHOR

Peggie Gallagher was born in Mayo and now lives in Sligo. In between she has lived in England, America and Dublin. Her work has appeared in many journals and books including *Poetry Daily*, *The Best of Irish Poetry, 2007* and *The John McGahern Yearbook*. She has been shortlisted for the Strokestown International Poetry Prize in 2007 and the Gregory O'Donoghue Award in 2011. She was winner of the Edgeworth Literary Competition in 2005 and of the Allingham Poetry Competition in 2000.

ACKNOWLEDGEMENTS

Acknowledgements are due to the editors of the following, in which some of these poems, or versions of them, first appeared: *Poetry Ireland Review*, *The SHOp*, *Southword*, *Cyphers*, *Scriobh*, *Badal*, *The Stinging Fly*, *Force 10*, *An Cathach*, *Cúirt Annual*, *Boyne Berries*, *Stand*, *Poetry Nottingham*, *Envoi*, *Orbis*, *Agenda*, *Iota*, *Peregrine*, *Atlanta Review*.

Thanks are due to Sligo County Council for a bursary to Annaghmakerrig.

Very special thanks to Patricia McCarthy, Geraldine Mitchell, Michelle O'Sullivan, Ann Joyce and Aoife Casby for their invaluable support and belief in my work.